PURPLE BOOK HYMNS

PRAISE FOR PURPLE BOOK HYMNS

"If you really want to know the prophetic heart and soul of a poet, just read what flows from their soul. Rev. Amiri Hooker has received a gift given by a beloved teacher, who saw in him a treasure despite his early childhood struggle with dyslexia and dysgraphia, and turned it into an even more amazing gift, as witnessed in this his latest published work. I strongly recommend and encourage you to read Rev. Amiri Hooker's continuing discovery not only of his voice but other voices that have been left unheard."

Bishop Leonard E. Fairley
South Carolina Conference of The United Methodist Church

"I've known Rev. Amiri B. Hooker since our Interdenominational Theological Center days (1995–1999)—he immersed in African thought, I in ethics and the craft of production. Even then, Hook's work carried the pulse of a people and the precision of a producer.

"*Purple Book Hymns* is that early promise fully realized: poetry, prayers, and litanies that read beautifully on the page, soar in the sanctuary, and translate seamlessly to the stage.

"From a production lens, this book is program-ready. You can lift pieces as spoken-word interludes, build choral call-and-response, score processional litanies, or design community sing-ins and festival moments around its texts. It's art with backbone—rooted in Black church tradition, alive with liberationist urgency, and crafted for intergenerational participation. The result is worship that breathes, performances that mobilize, and audiences that leave humming hope. From the poem "I Wish You a Mourning Christmas," I was hooked.

"His completely genuine voice rings through—ripe with imagery to be explored on stage, in sanctuary, and in community. And the non-rhyming litanies? That's the book's strongest lane—the clearest expression of his theological and social-justice voice. This is where his work will land hardest in the church and in society: giving people images to wrestle with, pulling them out of the boxes of their normal religious perspectives, and causing them to speak new words of life.

"If you curate worship, direct ensembles, plan festivals, or produce community arts, get this book—and get it in bulk. Celebrate its artistic impact by programming it throughout the year: Lent and Holy Week, Juneteenth and Advent, civic gatherings and neighborhood residencies. *Purple Book Hymns* doesn't just inspire; it equips. I commend it wholeheartedly to pastors, music directors, dramaturges, teaching artists, and organizers who want art that heals, gathers, and moves people to action."

Stephanie S. Scott
Arts Production and Management | Tri S Productions
(Atlanta/Decatur), specializing in theatrical production,
arts and music festival management, and
creative consulting for arts organizations

PURPLE BOOK HYMNS

A Pastor's Poetic Liturgy
of Poems, Prayers, and Litanies

Rev. Amiri B. Hooker

AdvocatePress

Advocate Press, Columbia, South Carolina

Copyright © 2026 by Advocate Press

First published in the United States of America in 2026.

Library of Congress Cataloging-in-Publication Data
Purple Book Hymns
p. cm.

ISBN 978-1-966237-11-2

This book is dedicated to my mother, Claudette Katrina David Hooker, whose honesty, humor, and devotion to the art of living shaped my becoming long before I knew how to name it.

It is also dedicated to my learning-difference teacher, Tonya Kim Austin, who—alongside my mother—taught me in the eighth grade that poetry is not a weakness but a power; not an accommodation, but a gift.

In a world that named dyslexia and dysgraphia as deficits, they helped me discover that language could still belong to me—that poetry could become a form of equality, a doorway into understanding, and a holy means of telling the truth.

CONTENTS

Powerful Spiritual Haiku

FOREWORD

Salvation—as a distorted cosmology—is rarely interrogated in our ecclesial circles. Too often, "to be saved" is framed as escape: a someday land where every day is Sunday, streets are paved with gold, and human striving is over. This end-of-time fixation captivates congregations, soothes anxieties, and props up the status quo. It is familiar in the church—and beloved by the oppressor.

Biblically, it's suspect. Theologically, it's thin. Practically, it's harmful. That narrow view has stunted ministry, muted prophetic voices, and withheld the love the dispossessed demand. We have seen the damage. We know better. And still, too many worship and work within this escape-hatch soteriology.

Rev. Amiri B. Hooker is not having it.

In these pages, Hooker offers new psalms and proverbs, poems and bars, lyrics and prayers—practical hosannas that are not mere "highest praise" but honest cries for deliverance. In the spirit of the crowd that processed with Jesus on Palm/Passion Sunday, this book calls for justice, liberation, and freedom now. This is not otherworldly flight; it is a grounded invocation. These pages cry *kumbaya*—"Come by here, Lord."

God's people need a fresh vision of salvation. Not God whisking us away to eternity, but God bringing eternity to earth. We pray it each week: that God's reign come and God's will be done on earth as in heaven.

Purple Book Hymns is a tool toward that end—liturgical helps that inspire courageous worship, encourage a distinguished eschatology, and move the church toward freedom, toward a foretaste of heaven in the world, toward a love that lifts every person.

Pastor Hooker has given the church a generous gift. Receive it— then use it, in the sanctuary and in the streets, to the glory of God.

Rev. Dr. Vance P. Ross
Co-mentor, Rooted: Anchored for Catalyzing Change,
United Theological Seminary (Dayton, Ohio)
Retired clergy, North Georgia Conference,
The United Methodist Church

INTRODUCTION

Welcome to a collection of ministry poems, life prose, and litanies from the little purple book of my life.

Growing up, reading and writing felt distant, being that I tested below grade level. In a learning disability class, a compassionate teacher guided me through the maze of dyslexia and dysgraphia. Today, I earn my living by weaving sermons, poetry, and prose one Sunday at a time. Ms. Kim Alston's gift went beyond teaching; it instilled in me a deep love for poetry, empowering me to interpret the true meaning behind the words on the page. This love paved the way for me to share wisdom, teaching children from my community during college summers in the reboot of the Children's Defense Fund's Freedom School.

Back in those days, my teacher gave me a small bound purple book and said, "Write in this whatever you want." I did just that, creating poems, word collections, and mind maps. I found the small purple book in some unpacked moving boxes recently and realized what an impact it had on my life—not only on my ministry career but in learning to express myself through the written and spoken word.

That's where the idea for this book began.

Within these pages lies not just a collection of poems but a testament to the transformative power of words. The discovery began as I found handwritten poems in cryptic script, so cryptic it defied conventional computer-scanning methods. Despite the challenge, an inner compulsion led to the translation of some of these passion poems, seamlessly kickstarting my current poetic expression.

Through this poetry, all born from dyslexia's challenge and hardships of culture, I share a message that transcends language, hopefully resonating with those who find solace and strength in poetic expression.

Welcome to a written world where faith and justice converge, transcending the limitations of priestly liturgy. As syllables and metaphors dance, words transform from hurdles into stepping stones. Navigating religion and justice, denomination, and biblical interpretations, the poetic lens becomes an expression of convictions, doctrines, and racial identity.

Each stanza is a prayer, and every line is a step toward understanding the divine interplay of church, Bible, faith, and the humanism sins that bind us all.

Rev. Amiri B. Hooker
February 2026

POETIC CALLS TO WORSHIP

CALL TO WORSHIP: SHAKEN

Based on Psalm 11:1-6

Leader: Beloved congregation, let us gather in reverence as we approach the divine presence of our Lord.

Leader: Just glad to be free, you know what I'm saying?

People: We've sought refuge in the arms of God, and in times of uncertainty, we shall not be shaken.

Leader: Just glad to be free, you know what I'm saying?

People: The bottom may drop out of the country, but our faith rests in the unchanging nature of our Almighty.

Leader: Take the shackles off our feet so we can dance, oh Lord!

People: We just wanna praise you! Lift the chains, and we will lift our hands in worship! Amen.

CALL TO WORSHIP: ARE YOU A KING?

Based on John 18:36

Leader: Brothers and sisters, reflecting on Jesus's profound words about his kingship, let us gather in worship.

Response: In the face of questions about his kingship, Jesus calmly declared, "My kingdom is not of this world."

Response: Let us lift our voices in worship, acknowledging the sovereignty of the one whose kingdom surpasses all realms. Amen.

CALL TO WORSHIP: BELOVED

Based on Leviticus 19:15-18

Clergy: Beloved community, "Don't pervert justice. Judge on the basis of what is right." We worship; let justice flow like a mighty river.

Laity: Lord, help us to live by your commandments. May we not show favoritism or spread gossip.

Clergy: Assemble in prayer, for we are called to be vigilant neighbors. Don't just stand by when your neighbor's life is in danger.

Laity: We confess any hidden hatred within us, O God. Grant us courage to address grievances openly and seek reconciliation.

Clergy: In our daily lives, let us uphold your decrees.

Laity: May our worship today be a commitment to walk in righteousness and unity, as we strive to live according to your word.

CALL TO WORSHIP: COMMITMENT

Based on Romans 15:1-5

Leader: Those of us who are strong and able need to step in and lend a hand to those who falter.

Members: May our worship go beyond mere words, finding strength in selfless service. Let us ask sincerely, "How can I help?"

Leader: In this sacred moment, as we join our hearts in worship, let each one of us consider the well-being of those around us.

Members: Our worship is a commitment to looking after the good of the people around us, genuinely asking ourselves, "How can I help?"

CALL TO WORSHIP: CHRIST'S BODY

Based on Romans 12:6-8 (MSG)

Leader: As we enter into worship, we are like the various parts of a human body. Each part gets its meaning from the body as a whole, not the other way around.

Members: Our worship is a celebration of being part of Christ's chosen body. Let us embrace our unique roles and functions, finding meaning in the unity of his body.

Leader: Let's just go ahead and be what we were made to be, without comparing ourselves with each other.

Members: Whether we preach, help, teach, or give guidance, let us do so with humility and authenticity.

Leader: In our worship today, may we keep a smile on our faces. Let the joy of serving and being part of Christ's body shine through.

All: Amen.

BIBLE-BASED POEMS

SYMPHONY OF BLACK
BIBLICAL INTERPRETATION

In the sacred realm where words entwine,
Black Bible interpretation, a dance divine.
Unapologetically canonical, a theological embrace,
Rooted in the soil of Black Americans' grace.
Socially located, a context bespoke,
Scriptures woven into Black life's cloak.
Listening keenly, the text's response unfolds,
Redirecting concerns, as ancient stories are told.
Patience, a companion in the reading chair,
Trusting blessings emerge with a careful stare.
Dialogue unfolds, a chorus of voices blend,
Black and White critiques, pathways to transcend.
Dialogue dances, a chorus of critique,
Black and White voices, in communion speak.
A quest for a richer reading, a shared embrace,
Black Bible interpretation, a harmonious grace.
In the symphony of Black biblical interpretation,
Unapologetic and theological, a sacred foundation.
Black and White critiques converge,
    forging a collective effort to attain
    a richer understanding of the sacred words.

DAVID'S SONG 3 & 1

Part I: Anointed Echoes
In the shadowed valleys of Bethlehem's heart,
A shepherd boy, anointed from the start.
David, a lyre's echo in the king's domain,
A brave soul, God's favor did sustain.

Saul's court echoed praises for the warrior's might,
Yet pleasure vanished with each ascending height.
Goliath's fall, a tale in fame's embrace,
Yet jealousy crept, a darkened, vengeful trace.

Part II: Murmurs of Foreskins
Saul sought a bond, a kinship in strife,
Offered his daughter, a desperate bid for life.
But David, humility clad, refused the prize,
Michal's love, a tangled web that ties.

A hundred foreskins sought in blood,
A gruesome bounty, as jealousy withstood.
Two thousand fell to David's might,
Saul's fear grew in envy's stifling night.

Part III: Psalms of the Heart
Mighty men rose, a legion in God's name,
David's army, a force no foe could tame.
From rooftop glimpses to a war-born sin,
Uriah's fate, a tale of darkness within.

Sweet psalmist of Israel, emotions uncurled,
David's heart, a canvas for the world.
In victories and falls, a shepherd's grace,

A pursuit of God, a heart's afterglow trace.

Promises lingered, a throne's eternal vow,
Jesus, the Messiah, from David's lineage, now.
In the tapestry of sin and redemption's art,
David, a man after God's own heart.

LYRICAL ADVOCACY

In the symphony of proverbs of advocacy,
Speak for the voiceless, the misfits' plea.
Justice's anthem, a stand for the poor,
A call that echoes real loud.

Samuel's verses, a cosmic ballet,
God's dance of life, a mysterious array.
From poverty's grip to the heights of wealth,
He/She lifts the fallen, restoring their voice.

Proverbs' field, a neglected stage,
Lazybones and slobs, a warning page.
A lesson learned from thistles and weeds,
A path to poverty where idleness works.

Revelation's vision, a poignant view,
Pain and poverty, an unyielding.
Yet, within the struggle, a wealth untold,
A divine paradox, a story with no royalties.

THE BOOK OF BEASTS
AND THE ANGELS

In the wilderness of forty days' stark embrace,
Tempted by Satan, with wild beasts in the race.
Angels ministered, a celestial balm,
Yet evil's whisper echoed, a haunting psalm.

Marked by the Bible's relay, the baton of evil passed,
From Eden's Garden to the ages, shadows cast.
Olympian runners, biblical writers in motion,
Life's dialectic, a cosmic ocean.

Life, a dance of hills and canyons wide,
Peaks of joy, plunges where sorrows bide.
A journey from festival to funeral, the Bible's theme,
Contrary winds, a pilgrimage, both harsh and serene.

Days touched by zephyrs of truth and justice,
Chilly breezes luring toward betrayal's abyss.
Peculiar profundity in its simplicity,
The Bible's attunement to life's complexity.

Hard passages, yes, but its essence is clear,
Basics spoken; we're all marred by sin's veneer.
"All have sinned," the fundamental refrain,
Born of woman, days filled with trouble's strain.

A book of idealism and fundamental truth,
Confronting existence with the vigor of youth.
The Bible, a mirror to our frayed reality,
Yet, in its pages, echoes profound vitality.

A LITTLE OF PSALM 119

Genesis, Exodus, Leviticus:
In the beginning, a whisper formed the earth,
Genesis unfolding, a tale of birth.
Foundational truths, relationships divine,
God's creation dance, his glory to shine.
Exodus tells of Israel's grand escape,
From slavery's chains, a history takes shape.
God reveals his name, his attributes bright,
Redemption's plan, a beacon in the night.
Leviticus, a manual divine,
For priests and Levites, a sacred design.
Regulations clear, a holy decree,
The king's earthly throne, set for all to see.

Joshua, Judges, Ruth:
In Canaan's land, where promises unfold,
Joshua's conquest, a story told.
Years of desert, the Israelites stride,
Fulfillment beckons, on Jordan's side.
Judges arise in moments of despair,
Crisis and apostasy, a recurring affair.
Leaders called by God, in tumultuous strife,
Restoring peace, the rhythm of life.
Ruth, a gem in the Judges' array,
A tale of faith in the darkest of day.
From fall to redemption, a lineage blooms,
David and Jesus, salvation resumes.

Psalms, Proverbs, Ecclesiastes:
The Psalms, a collection, centuries span,
Praises and prayers, a diverse clan.

Images vivid, in simile and metaphor,
Humanity's journey, God to adore.
Proverbs, a guide for the young and the wise,
Instructing the simple, a treasure that lies.
Knowledge and discretion, life's rewarding art,
Wise living's anthem, written from the heart.
Ecclesiastes, a philosopher's voice,
Limited perspective, life's intricate choice.
Under the sun, his musings take flight,
Human experience, in wisdom's twilight.

A LITTLE OF THE GOSPEL

Matthew, Mark, Luke:
Matthew, the Gospel of the Jewish kin,
Proves Jesus their Messiah, the sacred link.
Fulfilling scriptures, in life and lore,
A testament to faith, forevermore.
Mark's tale, a call in Rome's dark days,
Persecutions loom, and suffering sways.
Prepare, Mark says, for trials that come,
In Christ's footsteps, find strength to overcome.
Luke, defender of faith, with purpose grand,
Debunking falsehoods across the land.
Gentiles, too, part of God's grand scheme,
In Christ's teaching, their place supreme.

John, Acts, Romans:
John's Gospel unique, events untold,
A purpose clear, belief to unfold.
Jesus, the Christ, the Son of God,
Life in his name, the path to trod.
Acts, the bridge, from Gospel to preach,
Apostles' mission, God's truth to teach.
Continuation of Christ's earthly plan,
Establishing the church, a divine span.
Romans, Paul's letter of salvation's song,
Gospel for all, where all belong.
Jew and Gentile, in righteousness shared,
God's plan revealed, humanity repaired.

1 Corinthians, Galatians, Ephesians:
Corinth's problems, a sanctification theme,
Paul, a shepherd, guides the Christian dream.

Progressive holiness, a call to grow,
Love and unity, let Christian conduct show.
Galatians, a stand for faith profound,
Justified by faith, in Christ we're found.
No legalistic works, only grace,
In God's work, our sanctification's embrace.
Ephesians, no error to correct,
Expanding horizons, God's plan direct.
Dimensions of grace, high goals in sight,
For the church, a radiant, glorious light.

APPOINTED TO NINEVEH (UMC)

The tale of Jonah, divine,
God's call met reluctance,
A prophet, unwilling,
Nineveh Church
Yet God saw what God sees

Down in Joppa's harbor the address
Five members' divine recompense.
Encountering storm
   and Jonah,
Their lives transformed,

Jonah, rebellious, ran,
Through the unwilling,
Divine appointments,
   stories of grace
   untold,
Unrepentant,
   unmoved,
   God's hand at play.

In the dance, fishing the way.
It matters not
Divine appointments await.
For even in rebellion,
God's grace overwhelms.
So whether you heed or resist the call,
Divine appointments embrace all.

THE TRANSFORMERS' TALE

In the beginning, a promise divine,
He gave us power, his light to shine.
Sons of God, believers true,
Transforming lives, old into new.
Like caterpillars in cocoon's embrace,
Change unfolds, a gradual grace.
Obscure in slumber, destiny's keep,
Fragmented selves, chiseled by life,
Seek salvation beyond earthly strife.
Awake, oh sleepers, the time draws near,
Unveil the purpose, crystal clear.
A metamorphosis, a grand design,
The sons of God, in glory shine.
Awaiting the call from depths so deep.
"Awake, arise," the scriptures declare,
Salvation near, beyond compare.
Seek salvation beyond earthly strife.
Awake, oh sleepers, the time draws near,
Unveil the purpose, crystal clear.
A metamorphosis, a grand design,
The sons of God, in glory shine.
A journey through night to morning's dawn,
The transformation of a soul reborn.

CHURCH CULTURE POETRY

LEGACY OF THE FAITHFUL

In history's chapters, we churches stand,
Flagships of faith, shaping a non-united land.
Preserving culture, in hymns and prayer,
Anchors of identity, legacy with few members.

Empowering voices, social and political might,
From abolition to civil rights, a courageous fight.
Community centers, offering support and care,
In historic churches, a strong foundation laid bare.

Education's beacon in times of strife,
Nurturing minds, illuminating life.
Economic progress, entrepreneurship's seed,
In these hallowed halls, dreams take dreamers.

Healing spaces, resilience defined,
In adversity, strength and hope combined.
Flagship churches, pillars of unity,
A legacy echoing throughout eternity.

MEMBERSHIP SONNET 101

In Methodist halls where prayers ascend,
A call for justice, a sacred blend.
The church, a tapestry of diverse hue,
Racial justice, a mission true.

Stained glass windows, reflections divine,
In every heart, a sacred sign.
From pulpit to pew, the message spreads,
United Methodists, breaking old threads.

Love thy neighbor, a creed to uphold,
In the church's story, a narrative bold.
Racial justice, a hymn we sing,
In unity, God's grace shall spring.

WESLEY'S GREED

1908 the Methodist Creed was scribed,
A social call reverberating against unjust holds.
God's glory and good, our labor's aim,
Rights to property, a trust in his clauses.

John Wesley's wisdom, echoes profound,
Industrial winds, societal ground.
Riches beware, stewardship implore,
Greed's harm, a cautioning lore.

Prophetic witness echoes, as time unfolds,
A living wage anthem, the church upholds.
Moral budgets shout, prioritize the poor,
For in justice's name, God's children endure.

Wesley's voice through industrial hum,
Riches cautioned, stewardship drum.
Interconnected globe, wealth, and divide,
Human-made markets, under God's guide.

A living wage, in every industry's door,
Rights to organize, the Starbucks workers implore.
Steward money faithfully, moral budgets decree,
Prioritize the needy, over wealth's decree.

Wesley's whispers in the winds of change,
Industrial shadows, a world rearranged.
Beware the lure of riches, a stewardship call,
Greed's venom, a societal downfall.

Today global markets, complex and vast,
Human creations, God's judgment cast.

A living wage anthem, the church upholds.
Moral budgets shout, prioritize the poor,
For in justice's name, God's children endure.

Organized rights, for workers to be free.

MUSICIAN, DON'T SING PLEASE

In the echo of prayers, a soul's refrain,
Kirk Franklin's rhythm, Kanye's Sunday's gain.
In pews and pleas, a heartfelt plea,
A different vision for eternity.

"Preacher, take me to a higher plane,
Where rats of despair no longer reign.
No pit bulls feasts on dreams so dear,
In the gospel beat, let joy appear.

"Streets of gold, no need for those,
A celestial groove where freedom flows.
Not grand promises, but a humble creed,
A vision born of love, a radical seed.

"Families strong, united, and true,
Strangers embraced in the morning dew.
Gospel notes weave a soulful call,
Eternal fall, where spirits enthrall.

"No need for riches, no earthly gold,
For my soul's hunger, a story to be told.
In the paradise of loyalty's light,
Kindness reigns, the essence of the night.

"Dismantle the hymns of nationalism's tale,
Let unity and love prevail.
No ethereal promises or grand decree,
Just a realm where all are truly free.

"In Kirk's melody and Kanye's sway,
A Sunday morning, a brand-new day.

A fusion of faith and hip-hop's glee,
In this divine chorus, we find unity."

THE SHEPHERD'S CALL

In sanctuaries where echoes linger,
Black churches stand as figurines.
Pastors, shepherds of the sacred fold,
Beyond the pulpit, their stories hum.

Building trust, a pastor's sacred creed,
Communities united, a spiritual need.
With active reach and hands that serve,
In bonds of trust, their flocks preserve.

Addressing needs, the pastor's gaze
Socioeconomic disparities, the struggles
Tailoring ministries to specific hoes,
Empowering hearts as redemption flows.

Justice seekers, pastors arise,
Voices raised 'neath cathedral skies.
Against discrimination, poverty's cruel dance,
Their sermons fuel a transformation.

Holistic shepherds, hearts entwined,
Beyond the spiritual, life's ties
Job training, counsel, financial grace,
A pastor's love in life's space.

Bridging gaps in generational spans,
Pastors guide with loving hands.
Between the local and elders' plight,
Unity blooms, communalism.

Unifying force in every street,
Engaged pastors make bonds complete.

Coherence weaves through every thread,
A resilient ministry where all are fed.

In conclusion, the shepherd's role,
Extends beyond the pulpit's soul.
African-American churches stand,
Guided by pastors, within faithful bands.

PASTOR'S WIFE POEM
(HER, HE, THEM)

In a mountain retreat, 'neath skies so wide,
A pastor sought connection with a bride.
Ten questions framed, sincere and true,
To understand her heart, a yearly view.

How can I show love, make you feel adored?
Demonstrate appreciation, ideas explored?
Assure your heart's desires, make them clear,
A journey of understanding, year after year.

To make you feel secure, a fortress strong,
Address insecurities that linger long.
Confidence and joy in our future path,
Together we navigate, side by side, not apart.

Attributes to improve, practices refine,
Mutual growth, a goal we define.
Your joy, accomplishments that bring delight,
In our shared journey, a harmonious flight.

To be more like Christ, a desire profound,
Visible in prayer, in God's word found.
Sensitivity to sin, prompt and sincere,
Fruits of the Spirit, a life crystal clear.

Mutual goals, dreams we chase,
Together we conquer, in love's embrace.
A commitment made, on that page so signed,
In understanding and love, our hearts entwined.

POETIC HISTORY 601

COLOR OF COMPROMISE

"The Compromise," a revealing read,
In the journey through history's pages,
Exposing the church's role in racism's
Concerns linger,
Pair it with "Confronting Injustice,"
A struggle to confront,
Atrocities, a painful truth
Bible misused,
 a nation's wounds unsealed.

The church, Christ's bride,
 not as saintly
 hospital for sinners,
Complicity in racism exposed
"The Compromise," a truth to share.
Missed opportunities, a real haunting
Each era a redeeming dream.
Yet pride, fear, sin, a toxic blend,
Progress denied,
 a systemic vote must end.

Lynchings on church grounds,
KKK's pulpit echoes,

a dark travail.
Segregation,
Christian schools in defense,
A painful complicity,
   no recompense.
The biblical defense,
   a flawed translation,
Noah's curse twisted,
   a racial pretext.
Slavery justified, a perverse claim,
God's word misused,
   a church-based legacy of shame.
Faith's endurance seen,
Black Christians holding on,
   they clung to God's hand,
   a testament of endurance,
   is it faith or sin?

GONE NOT FORGOTTEN

1619, a year forgotten,
The White Lion's silent arrival,
A hidden chapter in history's tome,
Where Black lives bore an ancestral faith.
Mayflower's tale in every book,
But White Lion's shadow overlooked,
Symbolic erasure, a powerful statement,
Decided by those who mold history's placement.
In the land of freedom's proclamation,
Florida and Texas reject revelation,
1619 Project, banned by name,
Yet, in protests' unity, a different aim.
Structural roots exposed, not incidental,
A struggle against racial resentful,
Saving American history, a counteraction,
Two narratives challenging the nation.
In the echoes of a divided land,
A project's call to understand,
To reframe, redefine, and explore,
A nation's origin, our history to restore.

HALLS OF EMPOWERMENT
(FREE VERSE)

Within history's woven embroidery, Black organizations meet,

Free Masons, Eastern Stars, National Pan-Hellenic Council NPHC,
The Links, NAACP, Rainbow Push, PPC, Color of Change, Southern Poverty Law, united hand in hand. Pearls of empowerment, stretching o'er the land, cultural echoes resonate in sacred halls, a harmonious band.

From abolitionist fervor to rights' insistent demand, pulpits transformed to podiums, where justice was meticulously planned.

Beyond prayer, a helping hand, a community manned,
Solidarity thrived in centers where unity expanded.

Education flourished in fields where opportunities were sown,
In HBCU classrooms, seeds of knowledge marvelously grown.
Economic empowerment, a town's flourishing crown,
Networking roots, stability renown.

Through slavery's shadow, segregation's stifling air,
Black organizations stood, sanctuaries offering repair.
Resilience sculpted in each pew,
A legacy etched in the strength they knew.

SOCIAL JUSTICE MISSION

In the echoes of Jeremiah's plea,
A divine call to act justly, set free.
Oppressors' grip, unyielding and tight,
Social justice, a beacon of righteous light.

Psalmist's verses, a chorus so clear,
Happy are those, justice held dear.
Foundations laid in righteousness bold,
A prophetic measure, the truth to uphold.

In Zion's core, a stone foundation laid,
A line of justice, a plummet cascade.
Prophetic truths, in Psalms they reside,
Social justice, as God's own guide.

Responsibility bestowed on the high,
Governance weighed, decisions nigh.
Weil's virtue, supernatural grace,
Equality's cloak, in justice we embrace.

DON'T TAKE ME 2 DA KING (MLK 50)

In realms where crowns bring heavy fate,
A throne bears burdens, a tempting weight.
For Jesus sought a kingdom's embrace,
Yet thorns and crosses marked his place.

Michael danced in pop's royal attire,
But whispers of shadows fueled the fire.
Tupac, the hip-hop monarch's decree,
MLK all met a fate cast in tragedy.

Jam Master Jay walked with the rap king's grace,
A journey cut short, a haunting case.
Fresh Prince ventured to tennis's throne,
A kingdom elusive, trials unknown.

The King of Glory, a celestial tale,
Where earthly crowns often frail.
Don't Take Me 2 Da Kings, the perils sing,
No scepter for me, just echoes of a "no king."

RALLY, PROTEST, OR MARCH

In '81, we marched, hearts afire,
Dreaming of celebration, honoring a king's legacy,
Voices raised, footsteps echoing,
A vision of unity, a chorus of hope.

In '92, the streets roared with anger,
King riots and disturbances, chaos unleashed,
Yet amid the turmoil, seeds of change planted,
A community rising, resilient and strong.

A million men converged in '95, a mighty wave,
Defying the shadows of oppression,
Their march, a declaration, a testament,
To an African-American picture, painted with pride.

Fifty years later, as we gathered once more,
To commemorate a dream, not realized,
In 2017, White Right's ugly torches reared,
Symbols of division torn down, voices united.

With Rev. William Barber and Rev. Liz Theoharis,
We stood in defiance, in acts of civil disobedience,
Teach-ins, demonstrations, a symphony of resistance,
In 2018, our voices echoed from across forty states.

In 2020, for George Floyd, for Black lives,
We rallied, we protested, we demanded change,
Yet in city after city, police mishandled Black lives,
Their duty to protect, their hands stained with injustice.

And in 2021, a dark chapter unfurled,
Insurrection's specter haunting the Capitol,

A mob fueled by hate, seeking to topple,
The pillars of democracy, the fabric of our nation.

What lies ahead, Americans, this freedom time?
Another rally, protest, or march,
Where will our footsteps, apps, and megaphones lead?
In the journey Kin-dom, in the quest for no peace.

ECHOES OF HERITAGE

In the tapestries of oppression, a call emerges,
A plea for cultural resurgence.
Asa Hilliard and Amankwatia, architects of change,
In their words, a promise to rearrange.

Pan-African alliances, a call to unite,
Parents, organizers, in cultural fight.
Local, national, international lands,
Hand in hand, cultural work expands.

A socialization mission, not just a reply,
To oppression's grasp, a cultural ally.
A path laid forth, to development soar,
Preventing genocide, culture's C.O.R.E.

Pan-African alliances, a symphony of might,
Parents, organizers, in cultural flight.
Local, national, international keys,
Unlocking doors, where culture flees.

Ba Gallman and Ba Benton, seekers of truth,
In their quest, a resolute sleuth.
Before the chains, before the gloom,
A cultural richness now seeks room.

In Afrika's embrace, a narrative profound,
Of achievements untold, in history bound.
Philosophical echoes, scientific sway,
A stolen legacy, yearning to replay.

I WISH YOU A MOURNING CHRISTMAS

In the heart of America's Christmas,
echoes the somber refrain of the first yuletide,
A political system governed by wealth's cheer,

In America's Christmas narrative,
a somber note resounds,
Extreme poverty and widespread hurt,

In America's Christmas tale,
Where poverty and pain wove the fabric of life.
Political systems bowed to money's faithfulness.

Herod, a leader fearful of change,
Issued decrees causing innocent lives to rearrange.
Black and brown boys faced a tragic fate,

Black and brown boys, victims of systemic abuse,
Through police and judicial abuse, their lives in a
dire state. Police and judicial tactics, a tragic misuse.

No twinkling lights adorned that sacred night,
But the blood of innocent boys cast a sorrowful light.
A system issuing unjust decrees.

In Ramah, weeping and mourning,
Rachel's grief, a poignant warning.
Rachel's grief, a story unavailing.

The first Christmas was filled with collective pleas.
Is America's now a prophetic cry,
Is America's Christmas mourning?

WOKE CHURCH'S VISION

In Black Methodist pews, a revolution stirs,
A call for minds awakened, injustice incurs.
Woke, a term reclaimed, consciousness profound,
Seeing the dots connect, a cultural surround.

Urban apologetics' call resounds, urgent and clear,
A state of mind, a collective frontier.
Double consciousness, Du Bois's strife,
Moments of realization, a cultural life.

"Ephesians" echoes, awakened we stand,
Aware of sin's grasp, we challenge the land.
Woke, a term reclaimed, social awareness reigns,
Cultural, socioeconomic threads it sustains.

In Black Methodist halls, a clarion call,
Awakened minds no longer enthralled.
To issues of race and injustice, eyes wide,
Awoke from sin's slumber, no place to hide.

Prophetic preaching, a visionary art,
Seeing gaps, calling souls to impart.
Essentials clear, in the message of might,
Gospel-centered, clear issues in sight.

Curious observation, a probing light,
Defining by love, not exclusion's night.
Prophetic preaching, a bridge to span,
Forth-telling God's heart, a divine plan.

A SYMPHONY OF FUSION MINISTRY

In commission's charge, a symphony begins,
A fusion ministry, where faith and politics twins.
Traveling light, relying on grace's wings,
To present God with the people, not just things.

Poor People's Campaign, King's unfinished plea,
Against the triune evils, a call to be free.
Moderates challenged, a rift in the tide,
A movement born, in adversity, to abide.

In commission's light, a mission unfolds,
A fusion of faith and politics it holds.
Traveling light, relying on the grace,
To the towns, God's presence to embrace.

Fusion Ministry, threads woven tight,
Religion in action, in the American light.
Politics and public life, canvases vast,
For spirituality's brushstroke, a witness cast.

Fusion Ministry, groups unite with might,
Religion lived in the American light.
Politics and public life, avenues divine,
To exercise spirituality, the Gospel to shine.

Poor People's Campaign, King's sacred plea,
Rising against racism, poverty, militarism's decree.
A challenge to moderates, a call for change,
In the face of adversity, a movement arranged.

Public theologians, commissioned worriers rise,

Priestly authority, in truth and love lies.
Public theologians, warriors bold,
Priestly authority, a story to be told.

LIBERATION'S RHETORIC

In the echoes of Birmingham's jail, King's words resound,
A prophetic voice, mass gospel of truths profound.
White churches on the sideline, pious irrelevancies abound
Yet, in tri-pandemic's grip, the Black preacher is found.

Not only the bystander, but the oppressed church, too,
Allowing injustice to persist, a grievous rue.
Liberation, revolution, justice's plea,
Empty rhetoric without love's decree.

Love, the cosmic force, the arc's true guide,
Bending toward egalitarian creativity far and wide.
Democracy, liberalism, progressivism's call,
Mere slogans without love's enthralling thrall.

Empowerment echoes in the preacher's call,
A Sunday sermon, civil disobedience's sprawl.
Directed change, transformation's seed,
Black preacher's role in justice's creed.

Real-life empowerment, a practical tale,
Biblical teachings, a relevant trail.
In the pulpit's light, justice defines,
The Black preacher's sermon, empowerment's signs.

POWERFUL POETIC LITANIES

BEYOND THE PULPIT (BLM): A LITANY

In No Justice, No Peace communities,
Black Lives Matter, and churches stand tall.
Pastors, not quarantined to pulpit walls,
Extend their reach to where street protests call.
Response: In the echoes of street protests, we hear the call.

Trust, a bridge built with earnest care,
Pastors weave connections in the air.
Communities thrive with their embrace,
In civil disobedience, diverse souls find peace.
Response: In diversity's peace, justice and love embrace.

Addressing needs, a tailored touch,
Pastors delve into challenges that clutch.
Socioeconomic divides, racial strife,
Their ministries adapt, embracing street life.
Response: Embracing street life, a ministry unfolds.

Voices rising against injustice's tide,
Pastors who advocate stand side by side.
Amplifying concerns, a call to arms,

Community-led change, their sermons charm.
Response: In their sermons, the charm of change is born.

Holistic care in life's vast scope,
Financial wisdom, love to elope.
Job training, counsel, life's buffet,
Pastors guide through everyday fray.
Response: In life's buffet, their guidance lights the way.

Bridging gaps, generation to generation,
Pastors foster understanding, a revelation.
Unity blooms in their nurturing gaze,
A harmonious Black Lives Matter praise.
Response: In the nurturing gaze, unity takes its stand.

Unifying force in community's core,
Engaged pastors, a beacon forevermore.
Coherence in the tapestry they weave,
Strengthening bonds, hearts believe.
Response: Hearts believe in the tapestry they weave.

Black Churches Matter, beyond the pulpit's grace,
Pastors stand as pillars, in every place.
Black lives live when Black churches thrive,
Guided by pastors prophetic mattering lives.
Response: In thriving churches, Black lives truly thrive.

A LITANY FOR THE POORER

Black poverty,
Hispanic poverty,
Native American poverty,
Asian-American poverty,
and White poverty
Response: In the shades of poverty's lament, we stand united.

Amid the shades of poverty's lament,
Black, Hispanic, in varied incomes,
Unequal burdens from history's,
Where racial legacies echo loud.
Twice the likelihood,
Black and Hispanic, disparity nearby.
Thirty years pass, yet unchanged life.
Response: In the echoes of history, we confront the unchanged.

Black poverty,
Hispanic poverty,
Native American poverty,
Asian-American poverty,
and White poverty
Response: In communities where poverty dwells, we find strength.

In communities where poverty dwells,
White families navigate.
Yet Black and Hispanic families fight.
Within this first nation, a varied tale,
Poor White children, safer shores await,
Inequality's echo, a complex state.
Native and Asian host the unequal hymn,
Response: In the complexity, we seek justice.

Black poverty,
Hispanic poverty,
Native American poverty,
Asian-American poverty,
and White poverty
Response: In unity, we confront the unequal hymn.

In unity, we confront the unequal hymn,
For the Black, Hispanic, Native, Asian, and White,
Together we rise, breaking chains,
Demanding justice, equality's embrace.
In the unity of our voices, let justice roar,
No more the echo of inequality,
A symphony of shared humanity.
Concluding Response: Together, we stand against the chains of poverty.

A LITANY: THE COST OF LIFE

In a world of struggle, a single parent's plight,
Working hard for $14, under financial might.
Bills pile up, a delicate balancing act,
$800 biweekly, a meager income, in fact.
Response: In the midst of financial strain, we stand united.

Rent at $1,000, electrical, and more,
Car payment, insurance, an unwavering score.
Mathematics reveal a precarious dance,
Income meets bills, a slender finance.
Response: In the dance of economics, we seek understanding.

No room for extras, like groceries or phone,
A tightrope walks, precarious and alone.
A December chill, a power bill so steep,
$600, a blow, disrupting sleep.
Response: In the cold of adversity, we find resilience.

Facing eviction, courtrooms, and tears,
A judge indifferent, ten days, confirming fears.
A new place beckons, but credit is stained,
Eviction's shadow, prospects constrained.
Response: In the face of injustice, we seek justice.

Living in the car, with a child in tow,
Basic needs met, but life's bitter blow.
No billing address, a storage unit denied,
Surviving on bare essentials, pride set aside.
Response: In survival, we seek compassion.

Truck stop showers, gas station meals,
A desperate journey, life's cruel wheels.

CPS intervenes, the child is taken,
Job lost; judgment mistaken.
Response: In loss, we seek redemption.

Applying for homes, a waiting list so long,
Walmart job hunt, the struggle prolongs.
Car window shattered, belongings gone,
Summer's cold, despair carries on.
Response: In waiting, we seek hope.

Insurance adds burdens, a deductible high,
"High risk" label, clouds in the sky.
Homeless shelter, full and cold,
A tale of hardship relentlessly told.
Concluding Response: In unison, we pay the price.

BLACK PAPER LITANY: LITANY OF CONFESSION AND RESOLVE

Leader: We gather as a community, bound by faith and a shared history, deeply disturbed by the crisis of racism that grips this nation.

People: We acknowledge the pain, the struggle, and the unrelenting forces that seek to deny our humanity.

Leader: We, as Black Methodists, stand at the crossroads of history, knowing that our first response must be one of confession.

People: We confess, not in shame, but in the pursuit of truth, as we seek to confront ourselves and the world around us.

Leader: We confess our failure to fully embrace our Blackness—the beauty in our hair, our skin, and every God-given feature.

People: Too often, we have denied our Black beauty, seeking to conform rather than to celebrate the divine image in which we are made.

Leader: We confess that our service and ministry have not always met the needs of our Black brothers and sisters.

People: In our neglect, we have distanced ourselves, losing the connection that binds us as one people.

Leader: We confess that we have not always been honest with ourselves or with our White brothers and sisters.

People: We have often spoken in whispers, hiding the truth in order to maintain a fragile peace.

Leader: We confess that we have failed to boldly declare, "You have used your power to keep us down," both within and outside the walls of the church.

People: We have too often told others what they wanted to hear, instead of speaking the truth that would set us free.

Leader: We confess that we have not been significantly involved in the struggle for our own liberation.

People: We have allowed ourselves to be lulled into complacency, content with our "little world" and accepting our role as second-class citizens.

Leader: We confess that we have accepted the philosophy of racism for far too long.

People: In doing so, we have allowed others to define the terms of our existence, dictating when and how we should live.

Leader: We confess that we have accepted a false kind of integration, where the power has remained firmly in the hands of those who have oppressed us.

People: We reject this false peace and stand ready to reclaim our dignity, our power, and our rightful place in the church and in the world.

Leader: O Lord, hear our confession and grant us the courage to act, to speak truth, and to love ourselves as you have created us.

All the people: Amen.

THE FLAG AND THE CROSS: A LESSON ON LOYALTY—A LITANY

In the corridors of conscience,
A congregational or congressional vote
Perplexed minds grapple with currents untamed,
Restless, reckless, the world's narrative is on fire.
Response: In the flames, our loyalty is tested.

Tri-pandemic crises loom, casting shadows,
A global dance, a nation's battleground.
East versus West, spiritual ideologies at war,
Blood spilled on streets, rioters' strife's uproar.
Response: In the midst of strife, we seek understanding.

The haves, the have-nots, a social unrest,
A looming revolt, the forgotten oppressed.
Terrible conflicts, ideologies and poverty collide,
In the throes of crises, where does Jesus reside?
Response: In the collision of crises, Jesus is our anchor.

Russia's Israeli War, a global divide,
America's streets with racial tension tied.
Hunger's dart, a social malaise,
The forgotten masses 140 million US poor.
Response: In the division and hunger, we yearn for justice.

Western dissolution, dreams in jeopardy,
Fragments of hope, a pandemic mess
Will the American dream stand strong,
Or crumble, as the National Anthem is sung?
Response: In the anthem's echoes, our dreams stand resilient.

War drums echo, racial animosity's peak,
In hunger's silence, the voiceless speak.
Trouble reigns, a world in disarray,
In these crises, where is America's soul?
Response: In the chaos, we seek the soul's redemption.

Fearful for her, moral resources in test,
Survival's question, in the soul's unrest.
Yet hope persists in the darkest of nights,
For in the struggle, emerges church lights.
Response: In the darkest nights, the church lights the way.

LITANY FOR THE BLACK CHURCH: LIFT EVERY VOICE AND SING

Leader: Lift every voice and sing,
Response: Till earth and heaven ring.

Leader: Ring with the harmonies of liberty,
Response: Let our rejoicing rise.

Leader: Stony the road we trod,
Response: Bitter the chastening rod,

Leader: Felt in the days when hope banned had died;
Response: Come to the place for which our ancestors sighed.

Leader: We have come over a way that with tears has been watered,
Response: We have come, treading our path through the blood of the slaughtered,

Leader: Out from the stormy past,
Response: Till now we stand at last.

Leader: God of our weary years,
Response: God of our silenced tears,

Leader: Shadowed beneath thy hand,
Response: May we forever stand,

Leader: True to our God,
Response: True to our native land.

Leader: In the face of adversity, we stand united,
Response: For our roots run deep, and our spirits are ignited.

Leader: Black Lives Matter, a resounding cry,
Response: Injustice confronted, as we reach for the sky.

Leader: Black Church Matters, a sacred space,
Response: Where faith and resilience boldly embrace.

Leader: As we sing our song, through joy and strife,
Response: We affirm our commitment to love and life.

Leader: With every voice lifted, every heart ablaze,
Response: We march on, toward brighter days.

All: Amen.

POETIC PRAYERS
FOR DIFFERENT OCCASIONS

PRAYER OF CULTURES REMEMBERED

O Wise and Loving God, O Divine Weaver,

Your masterful hands have intricately woven threads of diversity, a medley of colors, cultures, and stories that dance in the grand mosaic of creation. Yet in the shadowed folds of our history, we acknowledge the stains of injustice against Aboriginal, Black, and various Asian communities. For the times when our eyes were veiled to the harsh truths of racism, when we faltered in action, we humbly seek your forgiveness.

Grant us, O Divine Weaver, the courage to confront discrimination that stains the fabric of our society. Instill within us a commitment to equality, a resolve to dismantle systems that perpetuate injustice, and the strength to resist complicity in the silent violence of privilege. Make us, O Lord, agents of justice, voices that echo the cries of the oppressed.

In moments of inaction, bestow upon us the gift of patience, an enduring flame that flickers in the face of adversity. As we navigate the intricate labyrinths of racial justice, may we be persistent advocates, unwavering in our pursuit of a world marked not by the scars of prejudice but by the radiant light of justice, hope, and solidarity.

In humility, we lay this prayer at your feet, trusting in your wisdom and grace. May your Spirit guide us as we walk the path toward a world where love reigns, where justice is not a distant dream but a tangible reality. We offer these words in the name of Jesus, the embodiment of justice and solidarity. Amen.

A PRAYER FROM THE BLACK PREACHERS' PULPIT

In the midst of, in the sanctuary, O Divine Presence, we stand, the Black preachers ascending the pulpit with a revered duty entwined. Our Black skin, a canvas etched with the struggles and strength of generations past. In the echoes of Nazareth's revolutionary son, we rise to the prophet's challenges, boldly confronting vanilla supremacy.

Clarion preacher, O Heavenly Guide, resounds against the might of oppressors and transcends mere rhetoric. Grant us the precision of a surgeon as we wield the word, dissecting the discomfort, laying bare the truth of "White fragility." In the hallowed silence, let our fervent prayers rise for Black Lives Mattering, a plea for acknowledgment and a call for justice.

Ancestors, revered and summoned, guide and inspire our words. Each uttered syllable, a vessel carrying the weight of earthly salvation, tracing a lineage from Wright's defiant curse to the voices unheard. Let revolutionary echoes reverberate through this sacred space, calling for victory against the shackles of injustice.

In these hallowed moments, let our proclamation be clear: Black lives matter—a declaration of existence, dignity, and worth. May the spirit of justice reign in our words, reaching the hearts of all who gather in this sacred space.

In unity and reverence, we offer this prayer, Amen.

PRAYER FOR THE COWARDS

Dear Ruby Bridges's God,

In moments of weakness, we seek your grace, O Lord. For those struggling with fear, doubt, and unfaithfulness, grant them strength to rise above their shortcomings. Guide the lost toward the path of righteousness, replacing vileness of white sheets with virtue, and offering redemption to those who have strayed.

May your mercy prevail over judgment, leading us to a life rooted in love and faith.

Amen.

PASTORAL PRAYER: BIBLICAL NARRATIVE FROM A TO Z

Gracious and Merciful Creator,

In the ancient Genesis of Exodus, we hear a resounding call—a call that transcends time and beckons us to be the voice for the voiceless, advocates for the misfits dwelling in the shadows.

Grant us the courage to amplify the chorus of the unheard. As we navigate the cosmic canvas painted by the Chronicles, 1 and 2 Kings, where divine rhythm plays from poverty to wealth, death to life, we recognize your omnipotence. You, the weaver of destinies, lift the downtrodden, breathe hope into burned-out lives, and restore dignity to those seeking a place in the sun.

Within the songs of Proverbs and Psalms, a vivid scene unfolds—a neglected field, a vineyard in disarray. Let the metaphor of consequences caution us against the allure of idleness. May we be mindful of the silent sermon in the fields, steering us away from the lingering houseguest of a dirt-poor life. Through resurrection, as promised in Mark, Matthew, Luke, and John, we find hope. Jesus, the shepherd, leads souls to the light—a beacon of freedom in the darkest night of both body and soul.

Revelation's revelation, please pierce through, unveiling the pain and poverty that persist. Yet, in this stark reality, a paradox emerges—a wealth unseen, challenging us to discern between truth and the façade of goodness.

O God, in this prayer, we seek strength to embody the call to justice, to stand with the destitute, and to weave a tapestry of hope in the face of poverty. May your guiding word lead us as we strive for a world where all your children live in dignity and abundance. In your hallowed name, we pray.

Amen.

BLACK CHURCH EMANCIPATOR PRAYER

Dear Heavenly Emancipator,

In this moment of prayer, we gather as the Black Church United Methodist, recognizing the challenges and divisions that we face in the twenty-first century. As we witness a surge in hate crimes and religious discrimination, we acknowledge the shortcomings of past separations in reducing racial and ideological tension.

Lord, we reflect on our history within the Methodist connection, from the early days with Richard Allen and Harry Hosier at the Christmas Conference. We remember the Methodist Church's antislavery stance, yet acknowledge the painful moments when White pastors resisted giving up their slaves. We lift up leaders like James Forman, who called for reparations, sparking a national debate on the responsibility of churches for their past roles in perpetuating slavery. We recognize the ongoing challenges highlighted by Michelle Alexander regarding mass incarceration as a modern form of oppression.

Lord, we confess that systemic racism persists in society and within our own church.

We appreciate the efforts of The United Methodist Church in addressing racism through agencies, devotionals, and webinars. Yet we recognize the need for a more profound response, urging the White church to move beyond silence and confront racism with depth and courage.

In this critical time, we pray for unity within the Black church as we stand to proclaim a Manifesto of Change and Deliverance. We are mindful of the divisions over LGBTQ+ rights, occurring amid a backdrop of rising anti-LGBTQ+ legislation and hate crimes. We understand that forces targeting various minorities are also directed at the church.

Lord, grant us strength, wisdom, and resilience as we navigate these challenges. May our manifesto be a beacon of hope, inspiring change and fostering unity within our community. Guide us, O Lord, in our pursuit of justice, equality, and love. Amen.

PRAYER OF PURPOSE AND THANKS

To the Architect of the Universe,

In this sacred moment, our prayers ascend. Gratitude flows like a wide river. Our prayers for each other overflow into thanksgiving. A chorus of gratitude to you, our Creator, and Jesus, our Messiah. Steadfast faith and love weave a building not made by human hands, uniting us in this divine space. Lines of purpose never grow slack. Hope guides us toward your divine plan, lighting our path through this journey of faith.

We pray that your unwavering message of justice echoes the same all over the world, bearing fruit, getting larger and stronger. May it flourish within our community, growing and strengthening hearts with the unifying truth.

Lord, work love into our lives through your Spirit, a testament to the truth of your message. As we continue this journey, may our purpose reflect your eternal plan. In Jesus's name, we pray.

Amen.

OPENING PRAYER: POOR PEOPLE'S CAMPAIGN

O God,

Grant us audience in this crucible moment. Grant us courage to confront injustices staining the moral fabric of society. Grant us the fortitude to lift the burden of poverty shackling the spirits of more than 140 million impoverished.

Protect the innocent, shield children from neglect storms, and let justice guard their dreams. In the sacred dance of civil and human rights, may no soul be left unseen and unheard. Grant us, O God, a Third Reconstruction, dismantling systemic injustice pillars. Address interlocking chains of racism, poverty, ecological devastation, the war economy, and distorted religious nationalism narrative.

Let our collective voice echo a harmonious symphony of:

Racial justice

Economic justice

Living wage justice

Health care justice

Ecological justice

Disability justice

Justice for the homeless

Justice for the poor

Justice for the low-wealth and working poor

O God, grant us sacred gifts to be architects of a world where swords become plowshares, where peace is our anthem. Grant us wisdom and courage to study war no more, weaving our shared humanity with threads of compassion, justice, and love.

Amen.

INVOCATION FREED DIVINE

O Spirit of Justice, come forth this hour,
With righteous power, break every chain,
In freedom's name, let justice reign,
Dispelling darkness with your holy power.

Embrace us, Holy Spirit, in this space,
Inspire our hearts to seek what's right,
Guide us with wisdom, dispel our plight,
As we journey toward your loving grace.

Grant us courage to confront oppression,
To stand for truth and equality,
In your presence, we find liberation,
A beacon of hope for all to see.

Come, Spirit divine, in this sacred space,
Fill us with your love, and mercy embrace.

PRAYER OF EARTHLY INVOCATION

To the God Who Is,

In the midst of life's uncertainties, we gather in your presence, guided by the words of Joel: "Fear not, Earth! Be glad and celebrate! God has done great things." As we embark on this sacred moment, we rejoice in the signs of your abundant blessings. "Fear not, wild animals! The fields and meadows are greening up. The trees are bearing fruit again, a bumper crop of fig trees and vines!"

Children of Zion, lift your hearts in celebration! "Be glad in your God. He's giving you a teacher to train you how to live right—teaching, like rain out of heaven, showers of words to refresh and nourish our souls."

Lord, as the rain nourishes the earth, may your teachings shower upon us, refreshing our spirits and guiding us on the path of righteousness. "Plenty of food for our bodies—silos full of grain, casks of wine, and barrels of olive oil."

We invite your presence to fill this gathering with abundance and joy. May your teachings be our guide, and your blessings overflow in our lives. In this celebration, we give thanks for the greatness of your deeds.

Amen.

INVOCATION OF LIBERATING UNITY

Grant us courage, O Spirit,
To confront the powers that seek to divide,
To challenge the systems that perpetuate inequality,
To stand with the marginalized and the oppressed.
Fill us with your love, your compassion,
Your fire that burns bright with righteousness,
Lead us on the journey toward true freedom,
Where all are seen, all are heard, all are loved.
Holy Spirit, come,
Justice and freedom abide,
Liberate our souls.
Amen.

VETERANS' DAY PRAYER

God of Love, Peace, and Justice,

It is your will for the world that we may live together in peace. You have promised through the prophet Isaiah that one day the swords will be beaten into ploughshares. Yet we live in a broken world, and there are times that war seems inevitable.

Let us recognize with humility and sadness the tragic loss of life that comes in war. Even so, as we gather here free from persecution, we may give thanks for those who have served with courage and honor.

Dear God, I pray for those who are in our presence who are either in active duty or reserve duty, and the fathers, mothers, siblings, spouses, and grandparents of those who are currently serving.

Dear God, we praise you for those who are willing to serve. Let all soldiers, Marines, sailors, airmen and Coast Guardsmen serve with honor, pride, and compassion. Do not let their hearts be hardened by the actions they must take.

Strengthen their families. Keep them surrounded in your love and peace.

Dear God, I pray for those who are in our presence who have served in the military in the past.

Dear God, we praise you for those who have served in the military. We thank you for those who put the welfare of others ahead of their own safety. Let us all be inspired by their self-sacrifice in service to those who needed protection.

Dear God, we praise you for those who have made the ultimate sacrifice. We ask that you comfort those who still feel the pain of their loss. Keep us mindful that you have promised to comfort those that mourn.

Dear God, we praise you for granting us these freedoms. Let us honor those who have served by working for peace.

Dear God, let us never forget those who have served. Let us never let go of your promise of peace. Amen.

A PREACHER'S PRAYER OF PROCLAMATION AND LIBERATION

In the echoes of resurrection, O God,
We stand at the intersection of faith and reality,
Where bullet holes mark the bodies of the martyred—
Trayvon, Tamir, Michael, Eric, Philando, Breonna—
Their wounds, like those of Christ, demand our touch.

Grant us the courage to be disciples anew,
To reach into the painful punctures of injustice,
To bear witness to the gospel of salvation,
Proclaiming liberation from sin and estrangement.
May our feet be beautiful on the mountains,
Heralding the good news of your reign, O God.

As Mary Magdalene ran with joy to her friends,
So may the I, the preacher, bear the weight of the gospel,
Charged to deliver the news of resurrection and freedom.
In this distinctive struggle for equality,
Guide our voices to uplift the disenfranchised,
For Sunday morning is a sacred release,
A time to let go and let God reign in our hearts.

In the spirit of Mary Magdalene, the apostle to the apostles,
May I, the preacher, stand as a beacon of hope,
A messenger of joy proclaiming, "I have seen the Lord!"
In this charge, we find our purpose and power,
For in the liberation gospel, we discover true freedom.

So let our preaching be a resounding declaration,
A testament to your love, justice, and unyielding grace.
In the name of the resurrected one, we pray. Amen.

POETIC BENEDICTIONS OF UPLIFT

ABOUT BENEDICTIONS

A benediction is a closing blessing spoken by a pastor to the congregation, acting as an encouraging word that indicates both the end of worship and an invitation to take God's love out into daily life.

Benediction: A Call to Compassion

We echo the cries of our broken world. As we go forth, may our hearts be attuned to the pain and struggles of others. In the face of unexpected death and profound disruption, let us be agents of love, justice, and grace. Empower us to challenge the lies that breed injustice and turn our nation toward the healing path of truth. As we confront the disparities laid bare by the pandemic, may we repent and seek a society that cares for the least of these. Strengthen us, O God. Use us, O God. Save us, O God. For we know that you are a very present help in the time of trouble. Amen.

Empowerment Benediction

In the face of challenges and attempts to silence, remember this: They try to shut us down, but it won't slide. The only fear we carry is of God, and with him on our side, our confidence is unwavering. As we depart from this hallowed gathering, go forth with the spirit that says, "You can't stop me and us!" Amen.

Benediction: Rising in His Image

As we conclude this blessed gathering, let us carry with us the transformative motto that echoes in our hearts: "No more mediocre, just getting by though." For we are created in God's image, resilient and enduring. Though we may have been down for a minute, today marks the day we rise. Let this be our commitment: to fight until we are finished. May the spirit of determination and the promise of God's image guide us in our journey ahead. Amen.

Benediction: Liberation Song

In the closing moments of our consecrated gathering, let the melody of freedom linger in our hearts. "I hear the chains falling, the chains are falling," resonates in the spirit of our shared journey. As we depart from this sanctuary, may the echoes of liberation accompany us. May the chains that bind us to injustice, inequality, and strife fall away. Hear it in the spirit, feel it in your soul—freedom reigns. Go forth, beloved community, carrying the assurance that the chains are falling. Amen.

Benediction: In Praise of the Creator

As we close this sacrosanct time of worship, let our hearts resonate with gratitude for the creator of the universe. Jehovah, whose hand shaped the earth and sky, has bestowed upon us the breath of life. May we carry the awareness of his divine presence into the week ahead. In recognizing the grandeur of his creation, may our lives become an offering of praise and worship to the one who is worthy of all honor. As we depart, may the spirit of gratitude guide our steps and inspire us to cherish the works of his hands in every moment. In the name of Jehovah, the creator, we pray. Amen.

Heart Benediction

As our hearts resonate with justice love, may the echo of heart love accompany you through the week. Let compassion and understanding be your guiding rhythm. Go in peace and love. Amen.

Intersection of Justice Benediction

As we stand at the intersection of justice and unity, let us receive this benediction inspired by the words of Rev. William Barber:

May the forces that seek to divide be met with the unyielding strength of solidarity. Just as the labor movement intertwines with the civil rights movement, so, too, may our hearts and efforts be intertwined in the pursuit of a more just world.

In the face of adversity, let us go forward together, resolute and undeterred. May the bonds that connect us be unbreakable, forging a path toward equality and righteousness.

As we navigate the challenges ahead, let the spirit of unity prevail, transcending any attempts to sow discord. Together, hand in hand, may we march forward, refusing to take even a single step back.

May the echoes of Rev. William Barber's call resonate in our actions, inspiring us to build bridges where others would erect walls. In the pursuit of justice, may we remain steadfast, knowing that progress is achieved when labor and civil rights move forward hand in hand.

And now, as we depart from this moment of reflection, let the flame of collective determination burn brightly within us. Amen.

Social Benediction

On this Sunday morning, bask in the glow of justice love. Walk the path of faith guided by the light of social gospel faith, knowing the divine resides within you. Depart with a spirit renewed. Amen.

Benediction of Dignity

Cloaked in the pride of Black dignity, leave this shared sanctuary with a testament to your worth and the worth of every soul. Carry the dignity of your heritage into the world. Amen.

Benediction of Liberation

With the anthem of Black liberation echoing in your hearts, break free from the chains of oppression. As you depart, may justice love propel you toward a world where the Black spirit is celebrated in all its glory. Amen.

Resilience Benediction

Our fear is reserved for God alone, and with his divine presence, confidence surges within. As we leave this space, carry the conviction that, no matter the obstacles, you can't stop God's gifts. Amen.

Resurrection Benediction:
Bearing Witness to Good News

As we prepare to depart, may our hearts be stirred by the echoes of resurrection, calling us to a sacred duty. Let us, like the disciples, embrace encounters with the resurrected, placing our fingers in the bullet holes of Trayvon Martin, Tamir Rice, Michael Brown, Eric Garner, Philando Castile, Breonna Taylor, and countless other martyred bodies. For molded by the crucible of racism and the unyielding struggle for equality in addressing the disenfranchised, our words become a balm, a refuge for those who seek solace. As we step into the week ahead, may our voices be instruments of healing, and may the rhythm of our proclamation resound with the truth, even in the face of injustice. Amen.

Benediction of Movement

Leader: As we stand on the precipice of moral revival, let our hearts be united.

Congregation: Forward together, not one step back!

Leader: In the journey of justice, may our steps be guided by the light of compassion.

Congregation: Forward together, not one step back!

Leader: As we strive for a world of equality, may our determination be unwavering.

Congregation: Forward together, not one step back! Amen.

POWERFUL SPIRITUAL HAIKU

ABOUT HAIKU

Haiku is a concise and traditional form of Japanese poetry. This verse aims to evoke vivid images, often drawn from the natural world, capturing a moment or essence in a minimalist yet impactful manner. Haiku have transcended linguistic boundaries, allowing for the creation of three-line poems in any language. The hallmark of a haiku lies in its brevity, adherence to syllabic structure, and a thematic focus, frequently emphasizing the seasons or nature. Lastly, haiku is fun, and this book ends with thoughts that seem to form leftover words and thoughts from the poems that live beyond the pages of this text.

Woke Church's Light

Awakened minds shine,
Cultural dots connect bright,
Prophetic preaching light.

Fusion Ministry Haiku

Commission's embrace,
Faith and politics entwined,
Witness in each step.

Roots Haiku

Augustine, Tertullian,
African roots, faith's legacy,
Guiding light shines bright.

Jazzabelle's Temptation

Jazzabelle's allure,
Entwining legs, sin's dance floor,
Souls trapped evermore.

Pastoral Embrace Haiku

Shepherds in the fold,
Community's heartbeat strong,
Pastors' love guides on.

Black Preaching Must: Three Haiku

Pulpit echoes truth,
Prophetic voice, challenges,
Black lives matter, hope.

Antiracism,
Dismantling structures of hate,
Ancestors' whispers.

"White fragility,"
In sacred spaces, they preach,
No earthly salvation.

Roots Resurrected

Cultural mission,
Pan-African hearts unite,
History reborn.

1619 Haiku Reviewed

Enslaved ship arrives,
1619, forgotten truth,
Legacy echoes.

Witness in Politics

Fusion ministry,
Faith and politics entwined,
Public witness shines.

Transformers Haiku

Caterpillar dreams,
Transforming in quiet faith,
Sons of God emerge.

Christmas Mourning Haiku

Wish for a mourning,
America echoes pain,
Herod's fear persists.

Justice UN Haiku

Divine command speaks,
Justice and righteousness reign,
Psalms echo the call.

Haiku in Three, in Worship

One . . .
Chapel whispers sing,
United hearts seek justice's
Sacred, timeless hymn.

Two . . .
Steeple against sky,
Racial justice in each prayer,
God's love never shy.

Three . . .
In unity's pew,
Methodist souls entwine,
Justice blooms, divine.

ACKNOWLEDGMENTS

I offer deep gratitude to Leonard Fairley, resident bishop of the South Carolina Conference of The United Methodist Church. Bishop Fairley's love for the written word—and for poetry in particular—has been a quiet but steady encouragement to me. His own poetic witness, *Who Shall Hear My Voice*, stands as a reminder that faith leaders need not abandon art to lead with clarity, nor abandon beauty to speak with conviction.

I also give thanks for Julius C. Trimble, who was elected and consecrated bishop by the North Central Jurisdiction in 2008 and retired on Sept. 1, 2024. Even in retirement, Bishop Trimble continues to lead with moral imagination, drawing on poetry as a source of inspiration while guiding the work of the United Methodist Board of Church and Society. His example affirms that justice work is sustained not only by policy and protest, but by language that keeps the soul awake.

I am profoundly grateful for the hands-on encouragement of James A. Forbes Jr.—renowned preacher, educator, and author, and one of the most effective voices in the English-speaking world. In the midst of hard conversations and demanding work within the modern Poor People's Campaign, he consistently offered me poetry—sometimes a line, sometimes a full verse—as both grounding and guide. Those moments reminded me that justice work, at its best, is sustained by spirit as much as strategy.

Finally, I offer sincere thanks to Jessica Brodie, Christian author, award-winning journalist, editor, and faithful encourager. She took the time—often and generously—to remind me to write boldly, to think beyond expected boundaries, and to trust that my voice mattered. Her affirmation helped me claim the freedom to tell the truth in my own cadence, without apology.

To each of you: Thank you for seeing poetry not as an accessory to ministry, but as a necessary language for faith, justice, and hope.

ABOUT THE AUTHOR

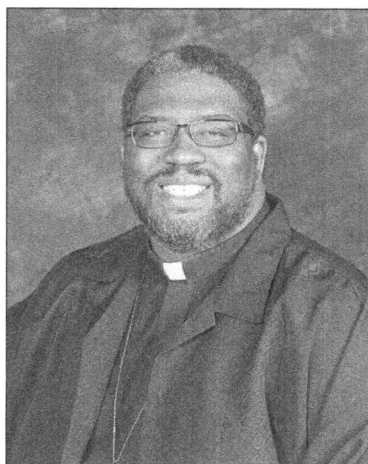

The Reverend Amiri B. Hooker serves as congregational specialist in the South Carolina Conference of The United Methodist Church, resourcing congregations in discipleship and community engagement. Hooker has served churches with a passion toward community organizing and social justice advocating. He has chaired and continues to advise the Advocacy Ministry Team of the South Carolina Conference and chaired the inaugural Racial Reconciliation Design Team.

A graduate of Methodist University in Fayetteville, North Carolina, and Gammon Seminary, he currently serves as a board member of the

South Carolina Christian Action Council. He is an active member of the National African American Ministers Leadership Council.

Hooker is one of the tri-chairs in the South Carolina Division of the Poor People's Campaign, working to build a broad, fusion movement that can unite poor and impacted communities across the state and target issues of voter engagement. He is a member and trainer for the NAACP (National Association for the Advancement of Colored People) and member of the executive committee of the South Carolina Caucus of Black Methodists for Church Renewal. He is the coordinator of the Southeastern Jurisdiction of BMCR.

He is also the author of *Preaching In the Midst Of . . . : How Black Preaching Has Changed in the COVID-19 Pandemic* and *My Banned Black History Sermons: Sermons about Jesus that Christian Nationalists Reject*, from the Advocate Press.

Twitter @Hookology.com
Facebook: https://www.facebook.com/Hookology
Web Page: http://hookology.info

www.ingramcontent.com/pod-product-compliance
Lightning Source LLC
Chambersburg PA
CBHW030846090426
42737CB00009B/1123